CANADA'S
150TH BIRTHDAY

Kathy Middleton

Crabtree Publishing Company
www.crabtreebooks.com

Crabtree Publishing Company
www.crabtreebooks.com

For my daughter Ava
May you remember Canada's sesquicentennial as fondly as I remember its centennial

Author: Kathy Middleton

Editor: Crystal Sikkens

Proofreader: Petrice Custance

Photo research: Crystal Sikkens

Cover design: Katherine Berti

Design: Katherine Berti

Print coordinator: Margaret Amy Salter

Prepress technician: Tammy McGarr

Explore more 150th Celebration projects at
www.150alliance.ca/projects

Check out the Government of Canada's 150th anniversary website: **www.canada.pch.gc.ca/ eng/1468262573081**

Photographs and Illustrations:
Alamy: Friedrich Stark: p 8; REUTERS, p 20;
   National Geographic Creative, p 31 (bottom)
Andy Chen/MCKids Academy (Canada150 in Minecraft): p 5
CNW Group/ParticipACTION p 27
Confederation Life Gallery of Canadian History: p 7
Getty Images: Roberto Machado Noa, Cover (middle);
   B Bennett, p 21
Ian Jacques/Delta Optimist p 24
iStock: © belekekin, p 22; © Micah Youello, p 30
Library and Archives Canada: Mikan p 13
NASA: p 23
Rob MacGregor: title page (Sesqui Dome), p 16 (Sesqui Dome)
Permission by Minister of Canadian Heritage: Canada 150 logo:
   pp 14, 16, 28
Shutterstock: © mikecphoto, cover bkgd; © wdeon p 9;
   © meunierd, p 12
Superstock: Design Pics, p 15
The Canada 150 Mosaic Mural for Baie St. Paul Quebec designed by
   Lewis Lavoie www.Canada150Mosaic.com: p 18
The Canadian Press: Nathan Denette, p 11;
   Justin Tang, p 25
Thinkstock: Jupiterimages, cover (kids in foreground)
Wikimedia: Creative Commons: pp 6, 10; Public Domain, p 23

All other images by Shutterstock

Library and Archives Canada Cataloguing in Publication

Middleton, Kathy, author
   Canada's 150th birthday / Kathy Middleton.

(Celebrations in my world)
Issued in print and electronic formats.
ISBN 978-0-7787-4108-4 (hardback).--ISBN 978-0-7787-4124-4 (paperback).--
ISBN 978-1-4271-1859-2 (html)

   1. Canada--Juvenile literature. 2. Canada--Social life and customs--
Juvenile literature. 3. Canada--Centennial celebrations, etc.--Juvenile
literature. I. Title. II. Series: Celebrations in my world

FC58.M55 2016   j971   C2016-906672-X
                                                 C2016-906673-8

Library of Congress Cataloging-in-Publication Data

CIP available at the Library of Congress.

Crabtree Publishing Company
www.crabtreebooks.com   1-800-387-7650

Printed in Canada/012017/TR20161124

Published in Canada
Crabtree Publishing
616 Welland Ave.
St. Catharines, Ontario
L2M 5V6

Published in the United States
Crabtree Publishing
PMB 59051
350 Fifth Avenue, 59th Floor
New York, New York 10118

Published in the United Kingdom
Crabtree Publishing
Maritime House
Basin Road North, Hove
BN41 1WR

Published in Australia
Crabtree Publishing
3 Charles Street
Coburg North
VIC, 3058

Contents

What is a Sesquicentennial?

Canada is turning 150 years old in 2017! A 150th anniversary is called a **sesquicentennial** (ses-kwi-sen-TEN-ee-uh l). Canada's birthday is celebrated on July 1 every year. This holiday is called Canada Day. Canadians get the day off to celebrate with parades, barbecues, and fireworks!

Canada is a country in North America. It has ten **provinces** and three **territories**.

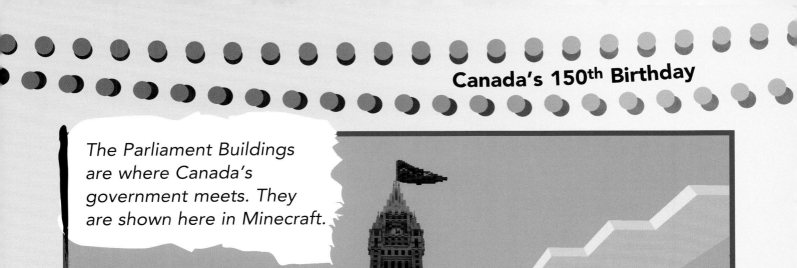

The Parliament Buildings are where Canada's government meets. They are shown here in Minecraft.

A sesquicentennial is a special birthday. It is a time to look back proudly on the country's achievements. Canadians are coming up with a lot of unique ideas to celebrate in their communities. In one project, children are helping to create Canadian buildings and events in **Minecraft**.

Did You Know?

You can visit Canada's national parks, historic sites, and ocean and Great Lakes **conservation** areas for free during the entire sesquicentennial year!

Confederation

Explorers from Europe started coming to North America in the late 1400s. France was the first country to claim land in what is now Canada. Britain was next, and both countries set up **colonies**. Eventually, Britain gained control of all the land.

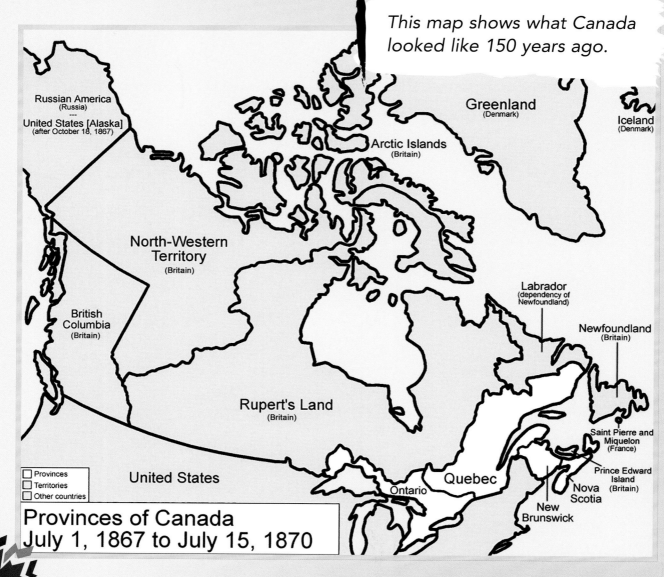

This map shows what Canada looked like 150 years ago.

Russian America
(Russia)

United States [Alaska]
(after October 18, 1867)

Greenland
(Denmark)

Iceland
(Denmark)

Arctic Islands
(Britain)

North-Western
Territory
(Britain)

Labrador
(dependency of
Newfoundland)

British
Columbia
(Britain)

Newfoundland
(Britain)

Rupert's Land
(Britain)

Saint Pierre and
Miquelon
(France)

□ Provinces
□ Territories
□ Other countries

United States

Quebec

Ontario

Prince Edward
Island
(Britain)

Nova
Scotia

New
Brunswick

Provinces of Canada
July 1, 1867 to July 15, 1870

Canada became a nation on July 1, 1867. This event was called **Confederation**. At that time, Canada had only four provinces: Ontario, Quebec, Nova Scotia, and New Brunswick. Other provinces joined the country as their populations grew.

At the time of Confederation, Canada formed its own government. Sir John A. Macdonald was elected Canada's first prime minister.

The Father of Confederation
RT. HON. SIR JOHN A. MACDONALD
P.C., G.C.B., D.C.L.

Did You Know?

In 1982, the United Kingdom (Britain) and Canada signed a new agreement that gave Canada complete control over its own rules and laws.

7

Indigenous Peoples

The first people to live in North America are called **indigenous** peoples. The Inuit are an indigenous people who live in the far north of Canada. This area, known as the Arctic region, is the coldest part of the country.

Many Inuit people still practice a traditional way of life. This boy is ice fishing.

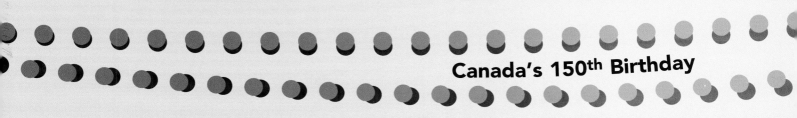

Powwows are gatherings where some First Nations people celebrate their heritage. This girl is performing a Shawl Dance.

First Nations are also indigenous peoples. There are many different nations across Canada. Each nation has its own language and **customs**. A third indigenous people, called Métis, has both First Nations and European **heritage**. They have their own unique **culture**.

Many Cultures

After Confederation, **immigrants** from around the world came to live in Canada. They brought the cultures of their home countries with them. A culture is the beliefs and habits of a group of people. Canadians are proud of their heritage and still celebrate the traditions of their cultures.

People often celebrate their cultural heritage on Canada Day.

Did You Know?

Being made up of many different cultures is called diversity, or multiculturalism. Canada is known as a multicultural country.

Canada has two official languages: English and French. This is because most immigrants came from Britain or France in the beginning. Over the past 150 years, immigrants from many other countries have chosen to leave their homeland to come to Canada.

Refugees are people who leave their homeland because it is unsafe. Here, Canada's prime minister greets new refugees from Syria who hope to become Canadian citizens.

When Canada Turned 100

The last big birthday party Canada threw was in 1967. The country celebrated its 100th birthday, which is called a centennial. The main centennial celebration took place in Montreal. The city held a world's fair called Expo '67. Over 50 million people from around the world came to the fair. The exhibits explored what the future would look like.

The United States' exhibit was a popular attraction at Expo '67. The building was shaped like a dome. Today it is a museum.

As part of the celebrations, an exhibit of Canada's history traveled across the country on a purple train called the Confederation Train. The train stopped in many cities so Canadians could see the display.

The Confederation Train is here

People stood in line for hours to tour the popular purple train.

Centennial Celebrations

Many **symbols** were created in honor of the country's 100th birthday. A song called CA-NA-DA was recorded with words in English and French. It was played all year long on the TV and radio. A centennial flame was lit in front of the Parliament Buildings in the country's capital city of Ottawa. It still burns there today.

St. Paul, Alberta, was named the Centennial Capital of Canada. One of its many fun projects was a **UFO** landing pad built for spaceships!

A centennial **logo** was created to mark the anniversary. It was a maple leaf made up of 11 equal triangles— one for each province and the Northwest Territories.

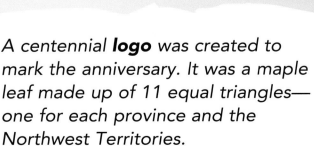

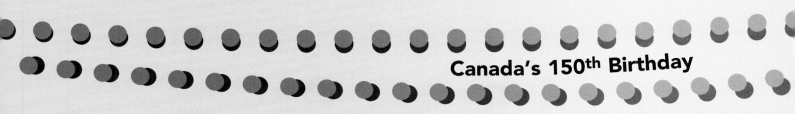

Did You Know?

Many Canadian communities joined in the centennial celebrations. Some groups recreated famous journeys and others built new buildings. Many did things just for fun. In Sudbury, Ontario, people built a giant nickel. In Nanaimo, BC, they held a race in bathtubs!

Sesquicentennial Celebrations

Exciting celebrations are planned for Canada's 150th birthday. A new maple leaf logo has been designed. It is made out of 13 diamond shapes representing all the provinces and territories. A festival about Canada, called SESQUI, will travel across the country inside a set of domes.

The SESQUI domes are round theaters where people can participate in activities, see live performances, and watch a movie called On This Land We Stand.

Hundreds of years ago, the only way to reach Canada from Europe was to sail in a tall ship. Forty tall ships will follow the same journey across the Atlantic Ocean in 2017. Called RENDEZ-VOUS 2017, the ships will visit all five Great Lakes and stop in 30 Canadian cities.

A tall ship has one or more tall poles, called masts. A mast holds up the sails.

Did You Know?

The tall ships will start in the United Kingdom, sail across the ocean, travel down the St. Lawrence River to Quebec City, then back across to France.

Community Projects

Many communities across the country are making their own special projects to celebrate. One group is asking 150 communities to create their own mosaic, or mural of painted tiles, to represent their city. All of the murals will be put together into one big mosaic of Canadian communities.

A mosaic from the city of Baie-Saint-Paul, Quebec, features the National Festival of Painting called Rêves D'Automne, *or Fall Dreams.*

In Ottawa, Ontario, kids from every province and territory are helping to build a playground in the shape of Canada.

Some groups are focusing on the environment. One activity, called the Our Canada Project, encourages children to come up with projects for treating the planet responsibly. Children can "pin" photos and a report about their project to a digital map of Canada.

Did You Know?

Volunteers in Peterborough, Ontario, will plant 150 pollinator gardens. This kind of garden grows certain plants that attract bees and other insects that carry pollen to other plants.

Other Milestones

Other **milestone** anniversaries are also being remembered in Canada in 2017. Canadians will be honoring the sacrifices made by their soldiers in World War I. The year 2017 marks the 100th anniversary of two important battles: Vimy Ridge in France, and Passchendaele in Belgium.

It is also the 75th anniversary of the Dieppe raid in World War II. A large number of Canadian soldiers lost their lives in the battle in France.

Canadians love hockey! The National Hockey League, or NHL, turns 100 in 2017. Canadians will be able to visit a special museum of their favorite sport. The hockey museum will travel across the country all year long.

Hockey superstar Wayne Gretzky will be the NHL's official centennial representative.

Did You Know?

Hockey's championship cup, the Stanley Cup, is also having a birthday. The Cup turns 125 years old in 2017.

150 Years of Change

The way we live has changed a lot in Canada over 150 years. In 1867, automobiles and airplanes had not yet been invented. People traveled by horse and buggy. By 1967, the computer had been invented but was not yet small enough to be used in the home. Today, people around the world are connected by the Internet, and some cars can drive themselves!

Today, we have 3-D printers that can print real objects, such as this model of a heart.

Canadians have been responsible for important inventions over the past 150 years, such as **insulin**, the telephone, and the robotic Canadarm tool (below).

Did You Know?

A science and technology exhibit called QUANTUM will travel across Canada in 2017. It is designed to encourage young people to get interested in science.

23

The Future of Canada

What will Canadians accomplish in the next 150 years? For the sesquicentennial, four themes have been identified as being important to Canada's future.

Diversity and Inclusion

Diversity means we are different, but we all get along. Inclusion means making sure people of all backgrounds and abilities are allowed to participate.

Rick Hansen's Access4All Barrier Buster project helps make schools and public buildings more accessible to people with disabilities.

Many Canadians are coming together to recognize the importance of supporting indigenous peoples.

Reconciliation with Indigenous Peoples

Reconciliation means to bring back respect and friendship to a relationship. Many indigenous peoples had their lands and traditional ways of life taken away when Europeans came to North America. Today, the Government of Canada has promised to work with indigenous peoples to strengthen and support their communities.

The Environment

We are responsible for taking care of the land we live on and protecting wild spaces. By doing this, it gives the people who live after us a chance to enjoy it, too. Volunteers in Nanaimo are focusing on this theme. Young people are learning farming skills and turning five acres (two hectares) of land into a community farm.

In 2017, Alberta will celebrate the return of the bison to Banff National Park. The Plains bison had become nearly extinct from overhunting.

ParticipACTION is a program that promotes physical fitness in schools. The program is challenging young people to complete a list of 150 activities in 2017.

Youth

Young people will be leaders in the future. That is why it is important to encourage children to learn about their communities and get involved when they are young. One project is hoping to inspire young people to do good things in their communities. A cellphone game called MC2 rewards you for your positive actions.

Join the Celebration!

How can you take part in Canada's 150th birthday? You could ask an adult to help you find the centennial song CA-NA-DA on the Internet. Use the same tune and come up with new words for the sesquicentennial. For any project, add the Canada 150 logo. Make a photocopy from this page and color the logo in.

CANADA 150

Research Canada's history and create a timeline. Mark the years each province and territory joined the country and other important events.

Look ahead to Canada's bicentennial in 2067. A bicentennial is a 200th anniversary. How old will you be in 2067? Make predictions, or guesses, about what you think you'll be doing 50 years from now. Why not think of a new tradition to start now that you can do every year.

One tradition might be to interview a different family member each year about the changes they have seen over their lifetime.

School Participation

To mark Canada's 150th birthday, try creating an activity for your class or school using the four themes for the future. For example, you could make a **time capsule** that holds four objects from your school that represent each theme.

You might decide to focus on one theme for your activity. If you choose the environment, you could plant a tree or start a vegetable garden at your school.

Your class or school could also join a project that is open to everyone across Canada. Explore the examples below and have fun celebrating!

A Kid's Guide to Canada— By Kids, For Kids
https://akgtcanada.com
Children in grades JK–8 can write a chapter for the guide introducing their communities to other kids across the country.

Art Tree Project
www.arttreeproject.ca
You can get a kit to make an art tree featuring your school, group, or special event. The goal is to get every town to have an art show featuring tree art.

31

Glossary

colony An area set up in one country but ruled by another country

Confederation A joining together of a group of provinces to form the country of Canada

conservation Care and protection of a threatened place or animal

culture The beliefs and habits of a group of people

customs The regular practices of a group of people

heritage The beliefs, customs, and traditions passed down from earlier people

immigrants People who move to other countries to live there

indigenous Belonging to a particular place by birth

insulin Medicine to treat diabetes

logo A design created to be easily recognized; often used in advertising

milestone A very important event

Minecraft A video game in which players build 3-D structures

province Land within a country that has its own government

sesquicentennial A 150th birthday

symbol Something that stands for something else

territory Land within a country that can make some of its own laws

time capsule A container that holds objects to be looked at in the future

UFO A sh_____ ____ ___d flying objec_____ ____ e

Index